Copyright at Edson Consultancy
Published by Edson Consultancy

Paperback 2020
ISBN: 978-0-9957468-4-8

All rights reserved in all media. No part of this book may be reproduced or transmitted in any form or by any means, electronic or mechanical, including photocopying, recording, or otherwise without the prior written permission of the publisher.

Teachers and parents are to use this book to gain the attention and make children understand the various positive emotions consist in it.

Active

Brave

Calm

Creative

Friendly

Kind

Loving

Proud

Silly

Thinking

Surprised

www.ingramcontent.com/pod-product-compliance
Lightning Source LLC
Chambersburg PA
CBHW060430010526
44118CB00017B/2434